RICHARD POUSETTE-DART

RICHARD POUSETTE-DART

The Centennial

32 East 57th Street New York

September 6 – October 15, 2016

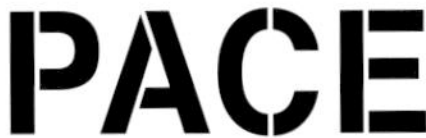

Richard Pousette-Dart

Martica Sawin

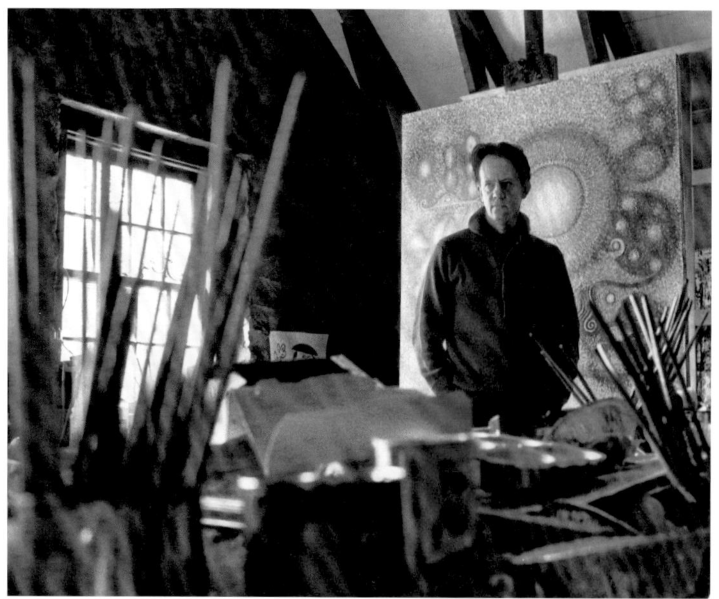

Richard Pousette-Dart in his studio,
Suffern, N.Y., early 1960s.

This exhibition marks the centennial of Richard Pousette-Dart's birth in 1916. His artistic output may be said to have started at the age of eight, when he drew and painted in his father's studio, and it continued until his death at seventy-six. A man of superhuman energy, driven by a compelling vision, and often working on a large scale, he left hundreds of paintings on canvas and on paper as well as sculptures, small carved brasses, boxes and boxes of drawings, and 220 studio notebooks filled with philosophical musings, thoughts on the role of art and the artist, drawings, practical reminders, and passages of lyric poetry, as well as pages blooming with interlacings of color and line like Celtic manuscripts. This large body of work was in one sense hermetic, in that it was the reflection of a personal system of belief that he began to evolve at an early age; yet there were also affinities with artistic, literary, and philosophical developments on the part of his contemporaries. Both aspects have been explored in numerous publications, including at least a dozen catalogues of Pousette-Dart museum exhibitions with essays by leading scholars, critics, curators, and poets, so that there exists a substantial body of perceptive writing on his art. However, there is much in his work that eludes verbal definition and needs to be absorbed directly on an intuitive level. The paintings chosen for the current exhibition provide an opportunity for the kind of meditative contemplation the artist had in mind when he wrote: "Great art leaves half the creation to the onlooker, gives the key to a creative experience. Draws the spectator into infinite mysteries."[1]

In my mind's eye I can still see Richard Pousette-Dart in his studio on the second floor of a fieldstone carriage house in a wooded area facing the foothills of the Ramapo Mountains. He moves slowly along the length of a horizontal canvas that extends between two easels. One hand holds a clam shell containing small mounds of pigment while a long brush in the other hand dabs paint onto the canvas with gentle deliberate touches. He seems to know how each addition will interact with what is already there, since he never pauses to step back to look at the effect of the accumulating points of color and or to gauge the amount of vibration generated by their interactions. Oblivious to the visitors talking in one corner of the studio, he continues the trancelike rhythmic motions of adding small points of pigment to the canvas. If at some point during the process someone suggests that the painting is perfect as it is he will respond that there must be layers beneath layers in order to arrive at a meaningful complexity, each layer requiring several days of continuous hard work.[2] To bring the canvas to the right pitch where all parts vibrate in harmony may require weeks or months of labor, a process he refers

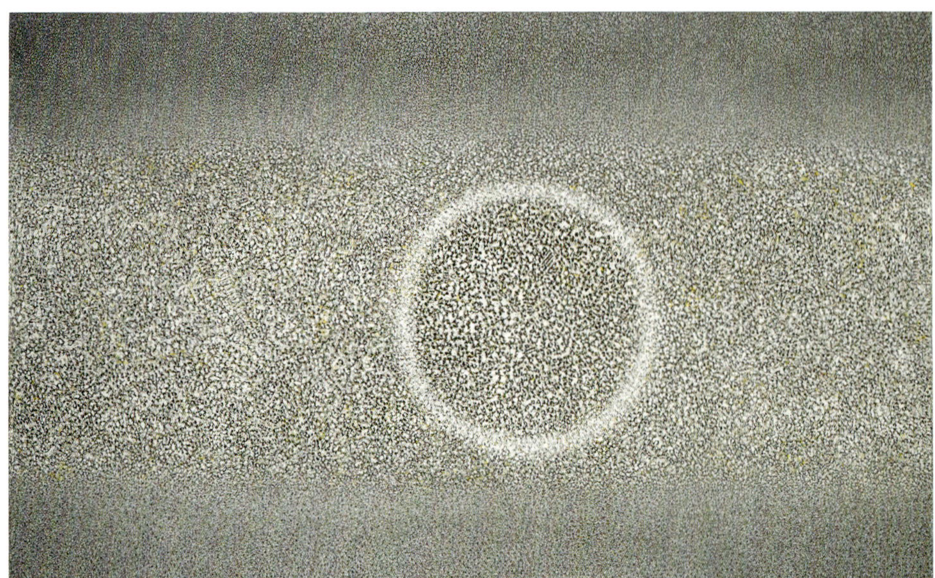

to as tuning. "Tuning" is the act of adding more and more touches of pigment, selected and distributed in such a way that myriad color interactions emit constant stimuli to the retina.

Later he stands beside a window in front of a small table where a blank sheet of heavy paper is laid flat. He takes up a brush, and without hesitating he outlines an almond shape that almost fills the paper, a shape that might be seen as a fish or an eye. The outlines become an armature as he fills in a mosaic of color. Asked about the significance of the shapes, he responds, "I love this shape. It holds the things within it and binds the things outside it; at different times it may mean something different. A painting is a thing within itself; it doesn't take its truth from externals."[3] The paint will be laid on in layers until, a few days later, the original shape will have vanished or become a faint ghostlike presence. As he applies paint he seems to become a transmitter of invisible energies to which he is impelled to give visible form. In turn, the canvas emits energies through light refracted from the pigmented surface. A sentence in one of his notebooks reads: "When the brush touches the canvas things happen that we could not know before and our preconceptions dissolve." In another notebook he describes his canvas as "an opaque transparency through which I look into the unknown."[4]

As he works, there is the accompanying sound through an open window of a stream running over its rocky bed close by the house. Sunlight filters in through the leafy green maze of the surrounding woodland, leaves that later will cloak the mountainside with a blazing mantle of red and yellow. In winter the mass of the mountain emerges, a stable presence seen through a filigree of bare trees; its profile is echoed in the horizontal division running through paintings such as *Presence, Ramapo Horizon* (1975 [fig. 1]). With the slow-motion changing of the seasons and the ongoing movement of the stream, a subliminal sense of time passing becomes part of the place. It's a secluded world, offering an immersion in nature, encompassing both the mountain's enduring mass and the stream's ceaseless motion, and a tranquility that enabled the artist to carry on the internal dialogue that fills the notebook pages and nurtures the fields for meditation that emerge on his canvases.

There was, of course, that other world to which he tangentially belonged, a world in which he had a place even before the genesis of Abstract Expressionism was underway—he was, in fact, an early contributor to that genesis. When he participated in the 1950 Studio 34 discussions that attempted to define the new art movement, he was already a veteran of nine solo exhibitions: at the Artists' Gallery (1941), the Willard Gallery (1943, 1945, 1946), Peggy Guggenheim's Art of This Century (1947) and Betty Parsons Gallery (paintings in 1948, 1949, 1950; and photographs and brasses in 1948). Among his fellow exhibitors in these galleries were many of the artists who appeared with him in *The Irascibles*, the *LIFE* magazine photograph that has come to define the nucleus of the nascent New York School.

In 1951 he lost the lease on his New York studio and, with his wife Evelyn and three-year old daughter Joanna, he moved to the hamlet of Sloatsburg, New York, and eventually to the carriage house on a former estate near Suffern that became their lifelong home. Although he continued to exhibit regularly, including solo shows at the Whitney Museum of American Art in 1963 and 1974 and a major retrospective at the Indianapolis Museum of Art in 1990, he remained aloof from the downtown art scene. When Red Grooms included him in a painting reconstructing a gathering of artists at the Cedar Bar, he insisted he had "never been in the place."[5] Being thought of as both "there and not there" might well sum up his relationship with the New York art world.

In contrast to most of the Abstract Expressionists who had been through some form of conventional art training and had passed through a phase of representational painting, Pousette-Dart evidently grew into his vocation at an early age in a household dedicated to the arts. Flora Pousette-Dart was a musician and a poet who encouraged her son's creativity, and his father Nathaniel was an artist, a successful art director, and author of books and articles on art. The surname adopted by his parents combined their family names, his father's Swedish and his mother's French. Much of Richard Pousette-Dart's life was lived according to early established idealistic principles. At fourteen he renounced the eating of meat or the flesh of any creature that had eyes to return one's gaze, a vow he never broke. As a high school senior he wrote a paper on pacifism and during the Second World War, unable to contemplate killing another being, he risked imprisonment by declaring himself a War Resister. His early notebooks reflect his thinking on the role of the artist. Around 1950 he wrote: "The true artist continually calculates the nature of the universe. He makes visible what cannot be seen."[6] This echoes a phrase from P.D. Ouspensky's *Tertium Organum*: "The artist must be a seer and make visible that which others cannot see."[7] If the theme of the artist/seer that recurs throughout Pousette-Dart's notebooks was part of the household conversation in his formative years, he did not mention it and he was wary of naming visionary writers he may have read. In his copy of *You Are the World* by Krishnamurti, who was much influenced by Gurdjieff and Ouspensky, there are a few underlined passages, including the following: "It is possible for the mind to recognize that the morality practiced in the world is not really moral at all; and in the understanding of that, the seeing of its envy, greed, and acquisitiveness, to be free of it without effort."[8]

His anti-war stand may have been reinforced by his admiration for the French-born sculptor, Henri Gaudier-Brzeska, who was killed in the First World War at the age of twenty-three, leaving a legacy of ground-breaking sculpture. Pousette-Dart's early sculpture and his animal drawings from the mid-1930s, as well as his small brass carvings all reflect his absorption with Gaudier-Brzeska, whose work he knew from Ezra Pound's book on the artist and from H.S. Ede's biography, *Savage Messiah*.[9] Most of Pousette-Dart's sculptures from the 1930s were done in plaster over metal armatures and have suffered considerable damage, but the one piece that he could afford to have cast in bronze, *Woman Bird Group* (1939 [fig. 2]), demonstrates a genuine command of strong sculptural masses and a rhythmic repetition of forms, as well as a link to the primordial images of iconic tribal art. Unable to afford adequate studio space to work on sculpture, Pousette-Dart increasingly turned to painting, but he continued to cut out small sculptures from thick sheets of brass, inspired by Gaudier-Brzeska's small-scale work in this medium. These he made throughout his life, often creating a piece for a friend to be worn as a kind of amulet. The continuing attraction of sculpture found an outlet in some remarkable wire constructions that he made around 1950, as he experimented with working in open-form metal, using processes that were transforming sculpture at mid-century. The few sculptures that survive and have been restored are cause for regret that he did not continue

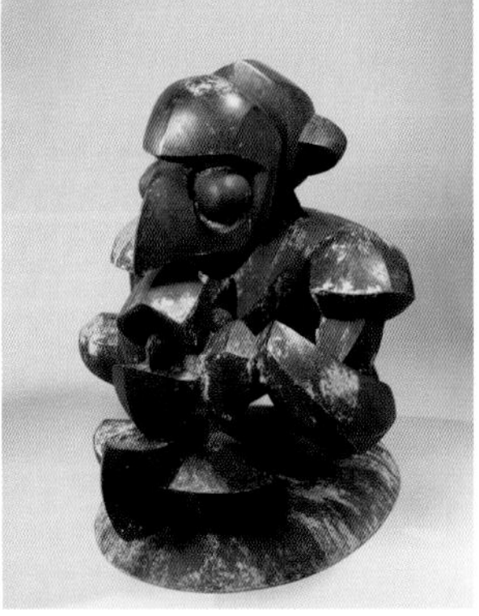

fig. 2
Woman Bird Group
1939
bronze, 24 ¾ x 19 ⅝ x 23 ⅞"
Smithsonian American Art Museum,
Gift of Mr. and Mrs. Frederic E. Ossorio

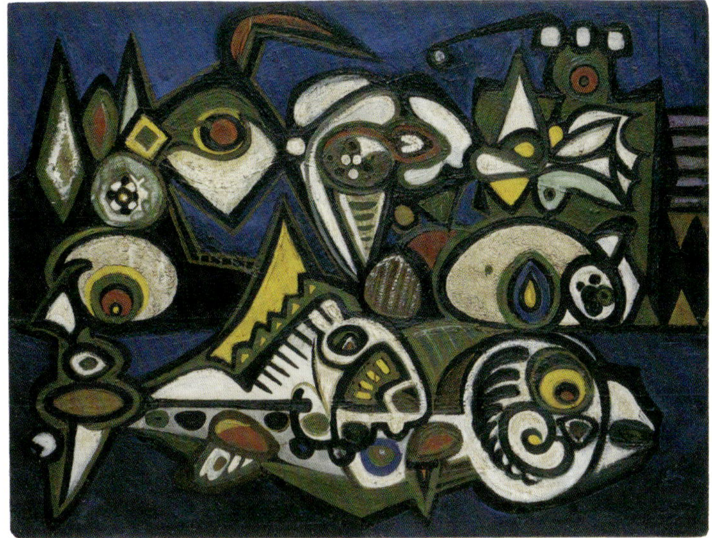

further work in this medium. A strong feeling for tactile, three-dimensional form remained an underlying aspect of his work, especially in the heavily painted surfaces where the paint sometimes stands up in peaks. As a kind of coda, late in life he began improvising sculptures out of whatever came to hand: string dipped in paint, egg cartons, styrofoam, perhaps in response to his urge to see the potential in ordinary materials.

The transition from sculpture to painting was made via boldly outlined totemic images, heads, fish, birds—some drawn from Northwest Coast tribal masks—interspersed with abstract forms.[10] Pousette-Dart never had to make the difficult decision to cross a boundary line between realism and abstraction. It came naturally to him to use his symbolic shapes—triangles, circles, spirals—to express his cosmic vision. These developed into mosaic-like, all-over compositions with heavy black lines binding the color areas like the lead channels for stained glass. Paintings such as *Bird Woman* and *East River* (1939 [fig. 3]) drew on the Pacific Northwest collections of the American Museum of Natural History, but also on his immediate surroundings. "I lived on the East River," he recalled of this period. "It was a big influence on my life. I loved the river, bridges, boats, fish, birds."[11] These paintings were characteristic of the work included in his first exhibition at the Artists' Gallery, New York, in 1941.

Having arrived at a synthesis between an abstract language and symbolic imagery, Pousette-Dart went on to unify his symbolic shapes by introducing a grid that provided a skeletal structure within which the shapes could function independently or interact across boundaries. Using shapes that had many differing allusions, including references to ancient origins, he expanded the grid to a canvas that for the time was of unprecedented size: *Symphony Number 1, The Transcendental* (1941–42 [fig. 4]). Because the grid could theoretically extend in all directions, it could be understood as a section of infinite space with a timeless array of symbolic references. This format was used in *Crucifixion, Comprehension of the Atom* (1944 [fig. 5]), to address a growing concern about the possible unleashing of atomic energy and its potential as a destructive force. Here he broke through the grid with undulating forms and used the dominating vertical of the cross to convey a powerful impact that explodes as it intersects with the horizontal cross-piece. By this time, Pousette-Dart was knowledgeable about atomic theory and the power that could come from splitting the atom. In the late 1930s he had worked for several years in a photographer's retouching studio where, through observing the enlarged granular structure of film, he came to realize that all form is made up of many points of light and that everything has a miniscule molecular structure. This awareness became an underlying current in many phases of his art and he referred frequently to his touches of paint as "points"—indicators of particles of energy.

The current exhibition starts at that mid-century watershed when Abstract Expressionism became an acknowledged force. The grid breaks apart in *Night World* (p. 16) of 1948, as white brush-drawn lines stand out graffiti-like over a black ground with luminous vistas. In *Gold Elegy* (1949 [p. 18]), lines give way to a scumbled painterly massing of gold tones emerging out of darkness. It is at this juncture that Pousette-Dart began to invoke "presences," usually a central

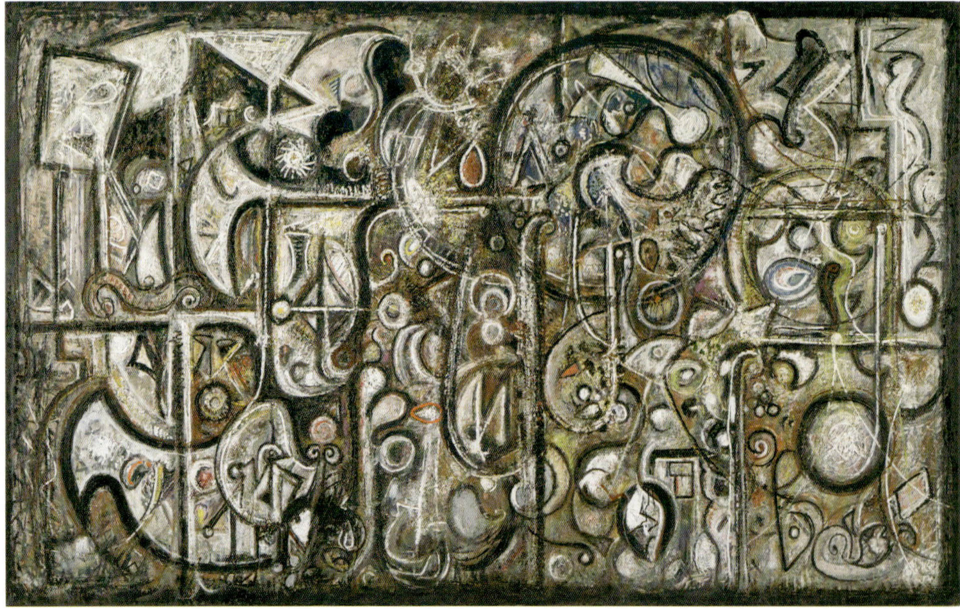

fig. 4
Symphony Number 1,
The Transcendental
1941–42
oil on canvas, 7′ 6″ x 10′
The Metropolitan Museum of Art, New York,
Purchase, Lila Acheson Wallace Gift, 1996

concentration of intensified brushwork that suggests a dematerialized force hovering beneath the surface. In some works it is barely perceptible, in others, such as *Presence* (1956 [p. 28]), a tenuous ghostly configuration appears to form out of a void. In 1955 the Betty Parsons Gallery mounted a remarkable show of his predominantly white canvases, for which he used titanium white grounds, overdrawn with a delicate tracery of fine graphite lines. Related to these are *Gothic #2* (1951–52 [p. 26]), and *Shadow of the Unknown Bird* (1955–58 [p. 36]), both of which explore the wide range of possible tonal variations in works restricted to black and white.

Interviewed in the 1980s, when he had a show of all black-and-white paintings, heavily painted in stark contrasts, he said, "People have different ways of creating limitations that will allow them to function. Discipline and liberation. Black and white puts you on the spot. It is the base of all visual creativity, an abstract quality; it's like an abstinence, a great dynamic balance to it."[12]

Increasingly in the 1960s, Pousette-Dart expanded and enriched his ways of handling paint, always driven by the urge to see what might be revealed in the "window to the unknown" that was his canvas. By 1966, in *Hieroglyph of Light* (p. 42), he was using a ground of small points of color combined with a tracery of white lines in a kind of abstract handwriting. The suggestion of minute specific shapes lends ambiguity, a sense of hidden meanings embedded in the cosmic reach of the all-over fluctuating color. There follows a succession of exquisitely subtle canvases, *Radiance #3* (1968–69 [p. 44]), *White Silence* (1974 [p. 58]), and *Presence Light* (1974–81 [p. 54]). The works of this period cannot be better described than in words from the

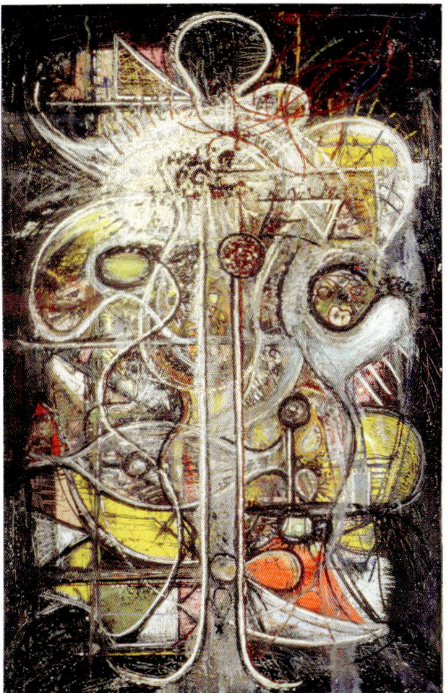

fig. 5
Crucifixion, Comprehension of the Atom
1944
oil on linen, 77 ⅛ x 49 ⅛"
J and J Collection

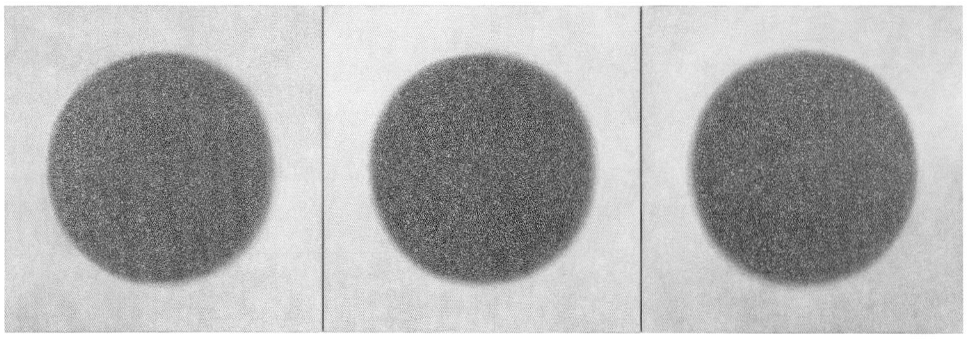

artist's notebook: "Form seen through light, millions of points of light, is forever resolving and dissolving, growing and being born and dying, becoming and disappearing."[13]

In the early 1970s, Pousette-Dart rented a floor in a rambling nineteenth-century factory complex in the nearby former mill town of Garnerville. There he worked on a large commission for the waiting room of the North Central Bronx Hospital. Reflecting on what emotional impact a 21-foot art work might have on anxious hospital visitors, he chose to paint two very different triptychs and let the hospital make the selection. The contrast between the two versions he produced is virtually a demonstration of his thinking about how the components of an abstract painting can stir the emotions as effectively as a realistic portrayal of tragic subject matter might do. *Presence, Healing Circles* (1973–74 [fig. 6]), ultimately chosen by the hospital, consists of three, equal size square panels, each with a circular center, radiating into a contrasting field of blue-tinged light. The stillness of the centrality is offset by the low key vibrancy of color and value contrasts both within and outside the circles. The hovering self-contained circles are centering, calming objects for contemplation with a reassuring completeness and sense of harmony. The long horizontal *Radiance* panels (27 feet combined length) have a stimulating, enlivening effect through the strong primary color, the multitude of swirling circles, and the pulsating set up by the myriad tiny points of light that appear to be receding into infinity (fig. 7). There is a joy to the lilting dance of linear motifs across the canvas.

A comparison of the differing emotional impacts generated by each triptych illuminates Pousette-Dart's musician-like use of tempo and tone to stir chords of response on the part of the viewer. The creation of these works is motivated not so much by a need for self-expression as by a desire to transmit an awareness of a vibrating cosmos into which all existence is integrated; it is immaterial whether one interprets it in scientific or religious terms. Because of the fluctuation of hue and value, the ambiguity of edges, and the refracted light from the textured surfaces, a Pousette-Dart painting requires continual retinal adaptation or extended seeing, as in listening to music. In this way, the works fulfill his goal, stated in so many ways in the notebooks, to achieve "living form, not hard edge, not soft edge, living form…edge of going on."[14]

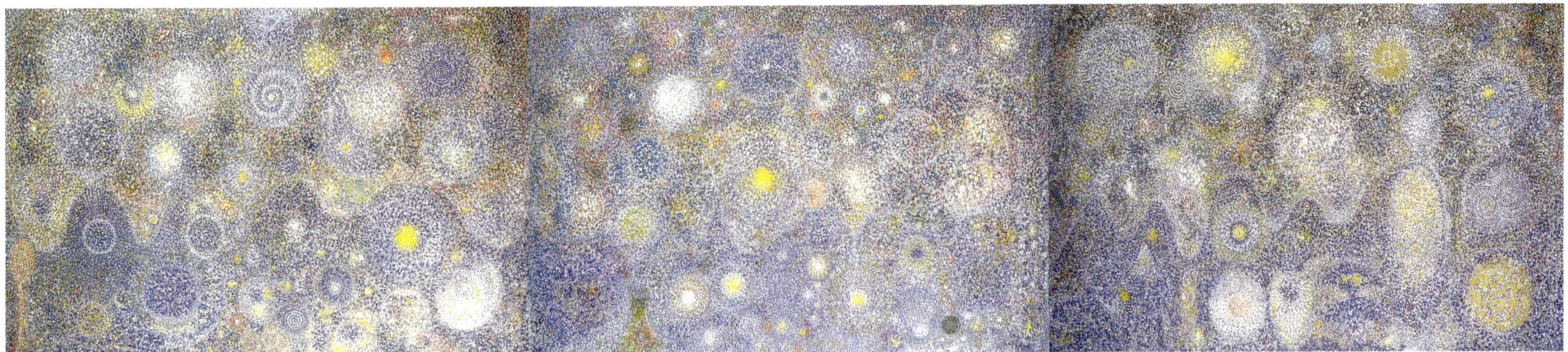

fig. 7
Radiance
1973–74
acrylic on linen, 3 panels
6 x 9' each
Private collection

1   Notebook B 176. Notebook numbers were established during the inventory of the artist's estate; dates are approximate.

2   Conversation with the author, late 1950s.

3   Conversation with the author in the studio, c. 1974.

4   Notebook B 176.

5   Artist's statement to author, c. late 1980s.

6   Conversation with the author in the studio, c. 1974.

7   *Tertium Organum*, revised translation (New York: Random House/ Vintage Books, 1982), p. 133.

8   Notebook B 97, p. 116.

9   Gail Levin first drew attention to the connection with Gaudier-Brzeska in her article "Richard Pousette-Dart's Emergence as an Abstract Expressionist," *Arts Magazine*, 54 (March 1980).

10   John Yau, "Impersonal Truths," in *Richard Pousette-Dart: Mythic Heads and Forms: Paintings and Drawings 1935 to 1942*, exh. cat. (New York: Knoedler & Co., 2003).

11   Conversation with the author, March 8, 1984.

12   Interview with the author, July 14, 1981.

13   Notebook B 186, 1950–60.

14   Notebook B 186, 1950–60.

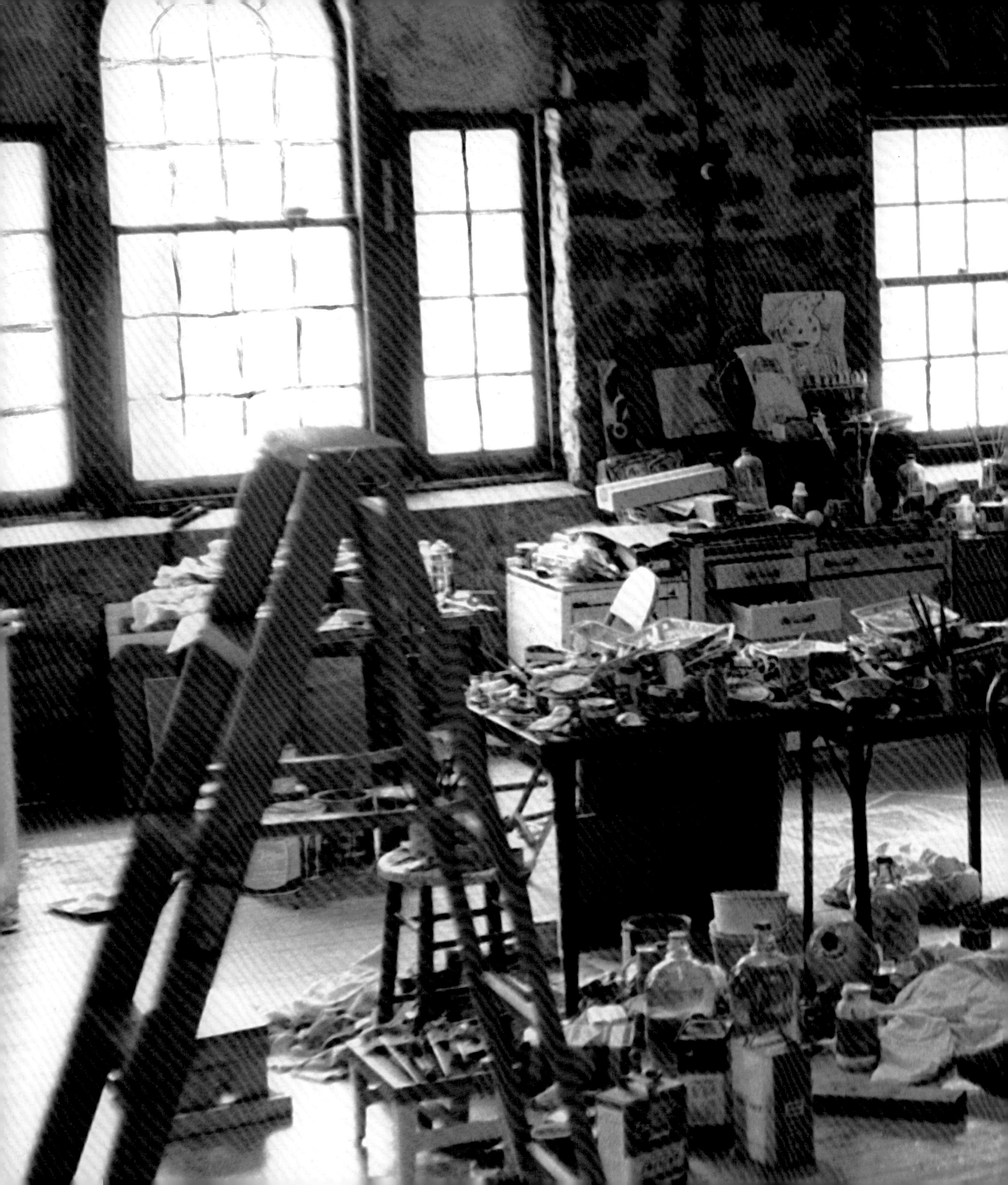

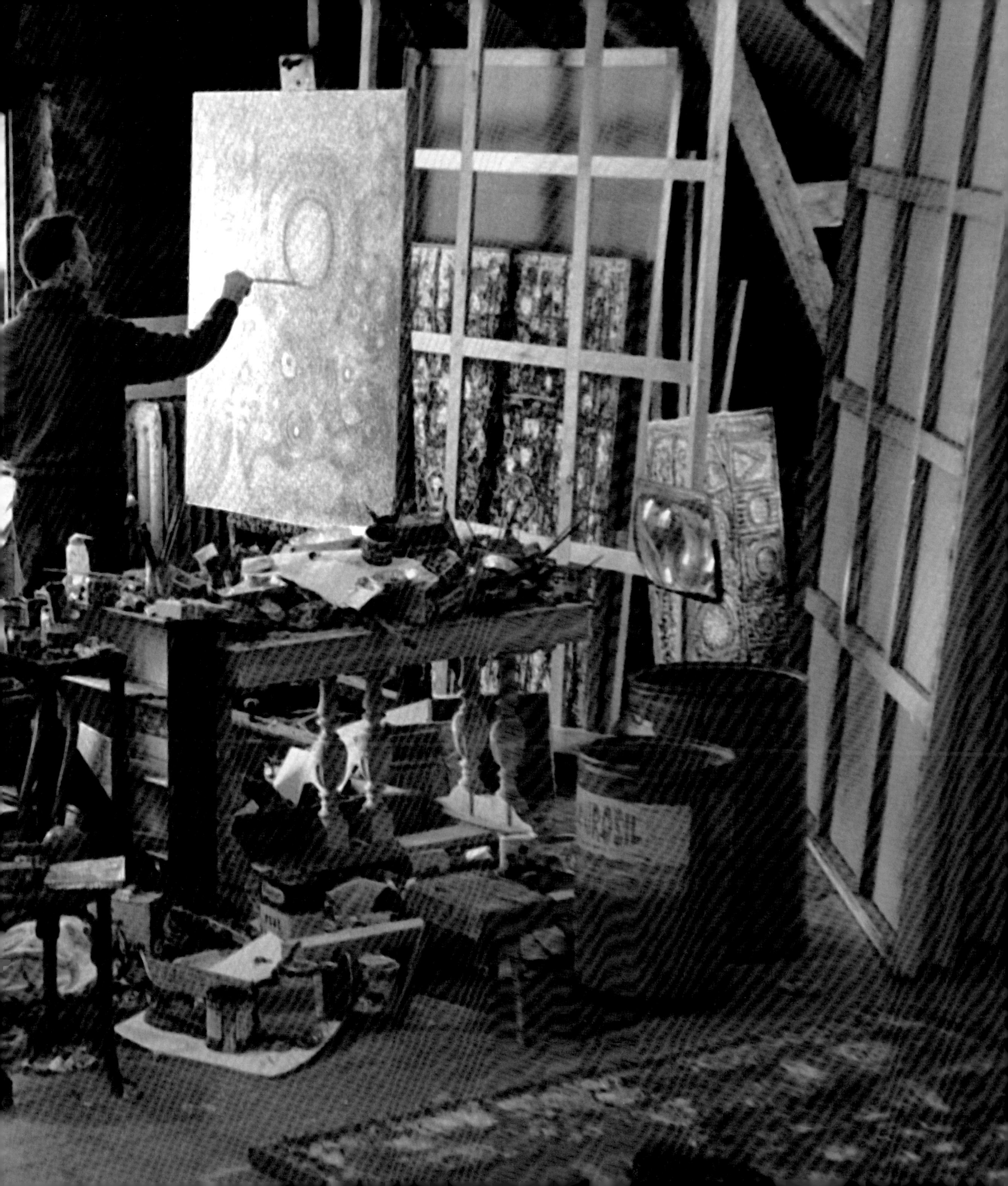

Night World

1948

oil on linen, 52 ¹/₂ x 62 ³/₄"

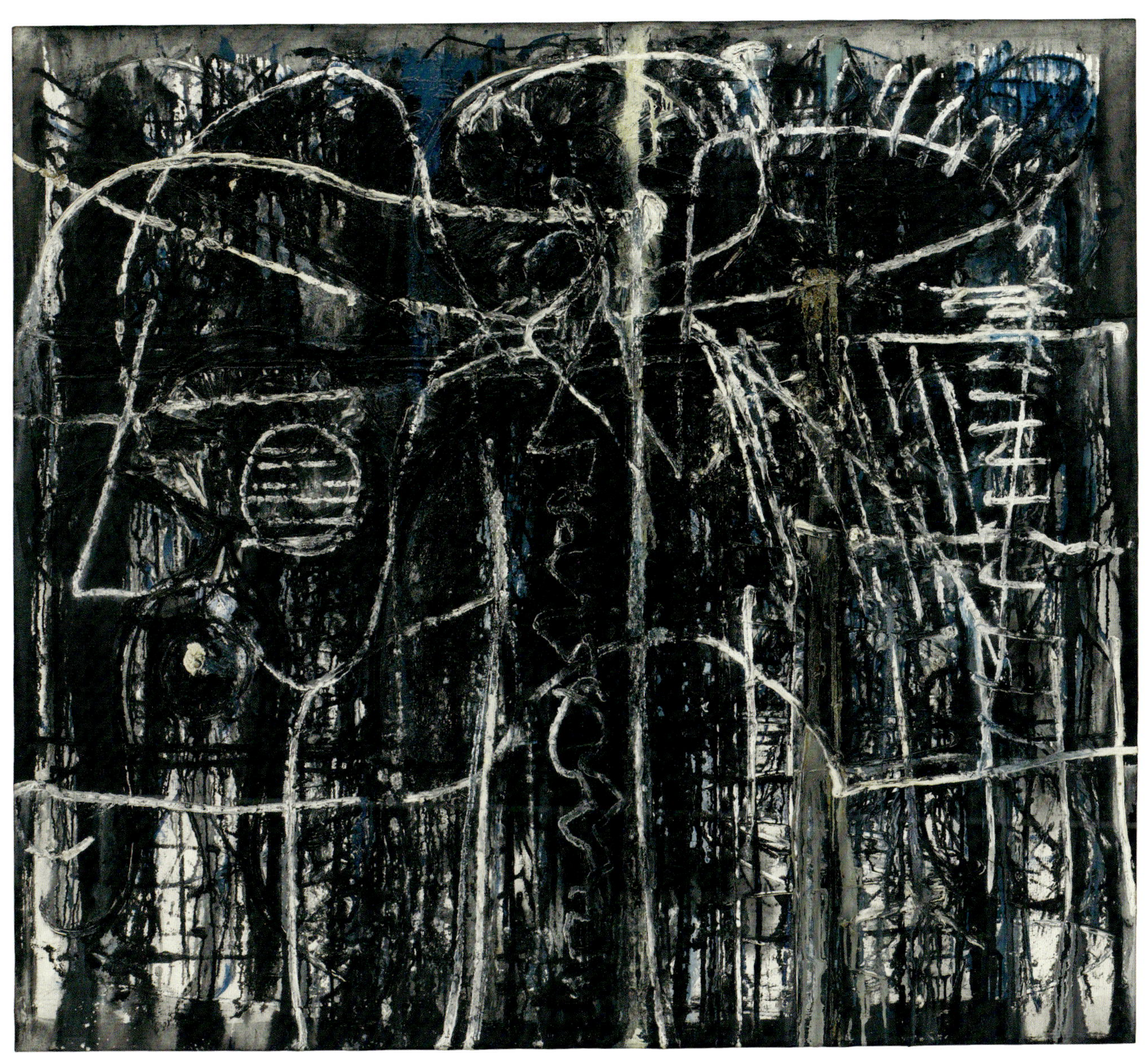

Gold Elegy

1949

acrylic and mixed media on linen, 48 x 41"

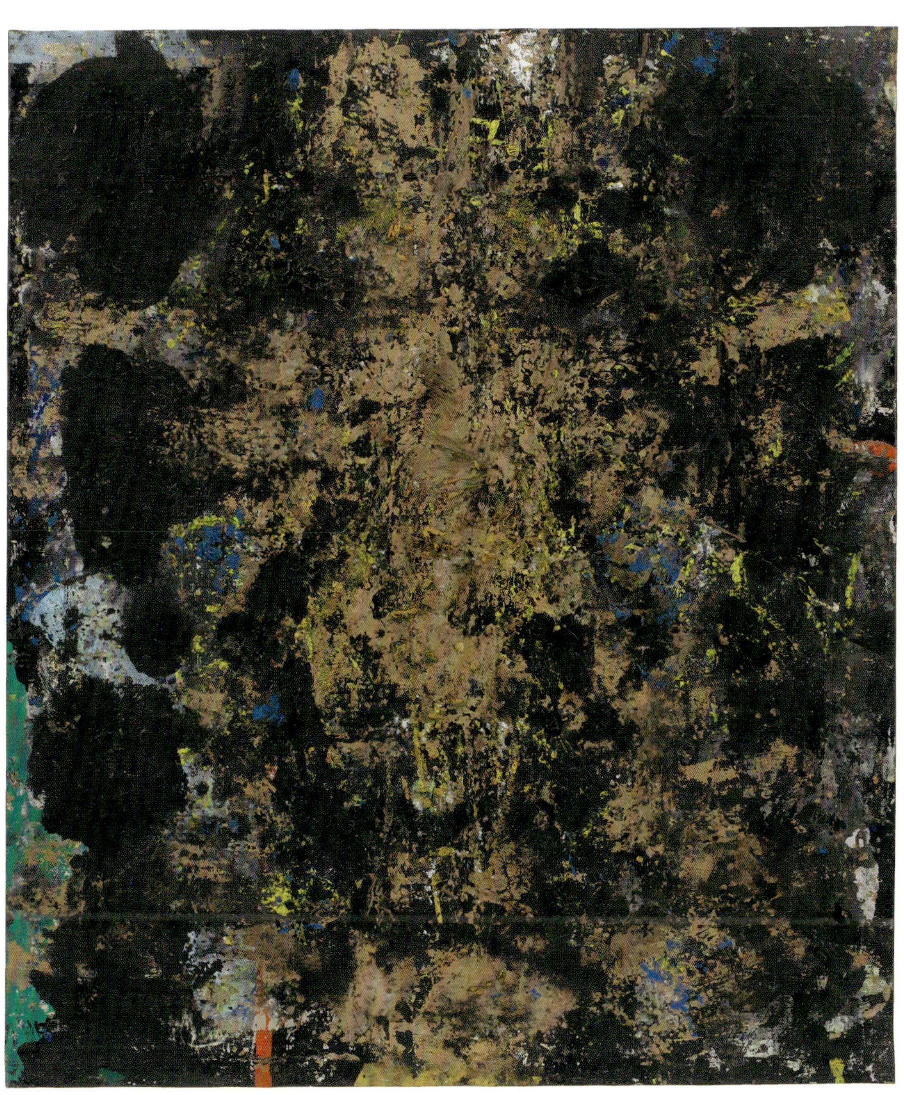

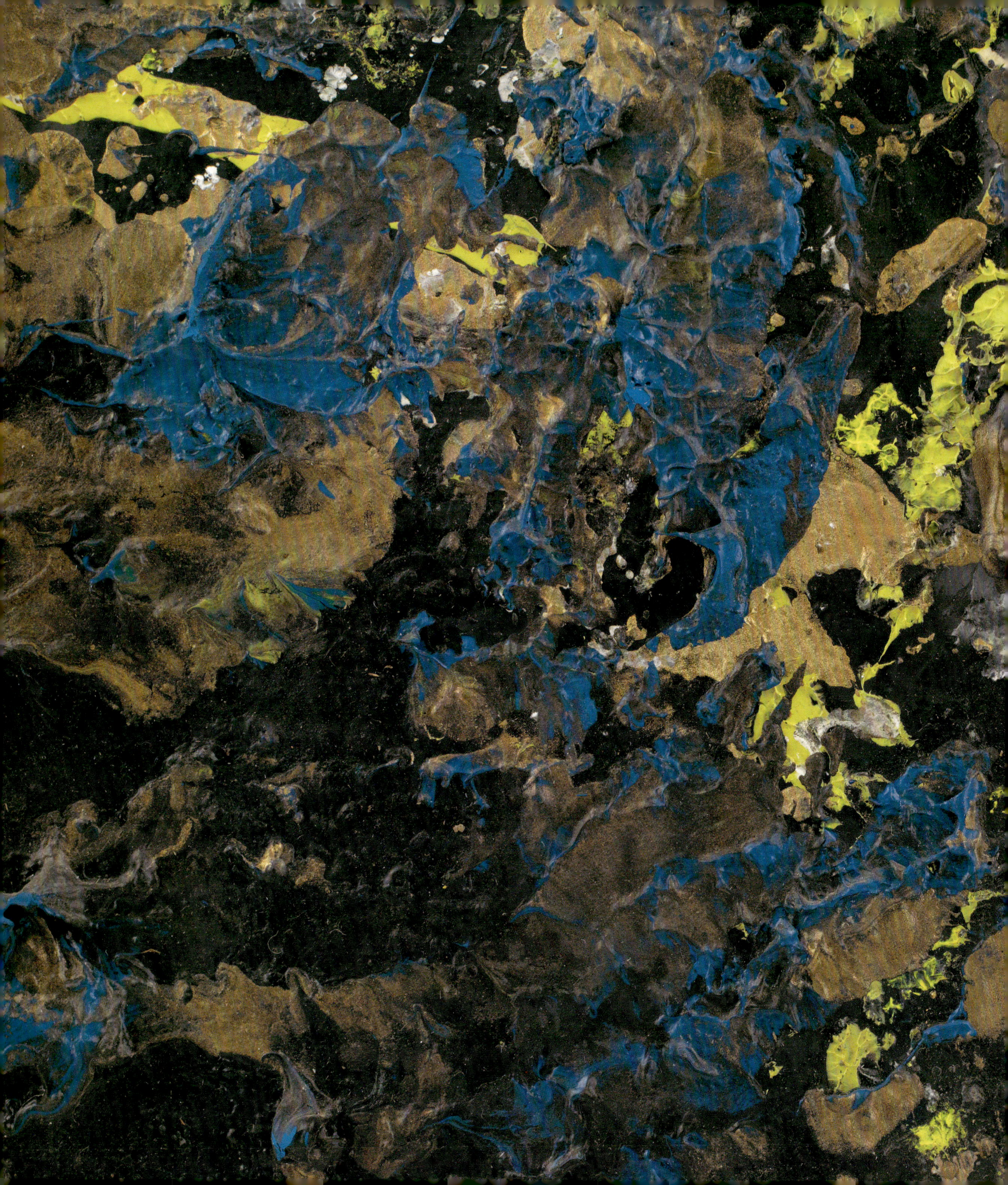

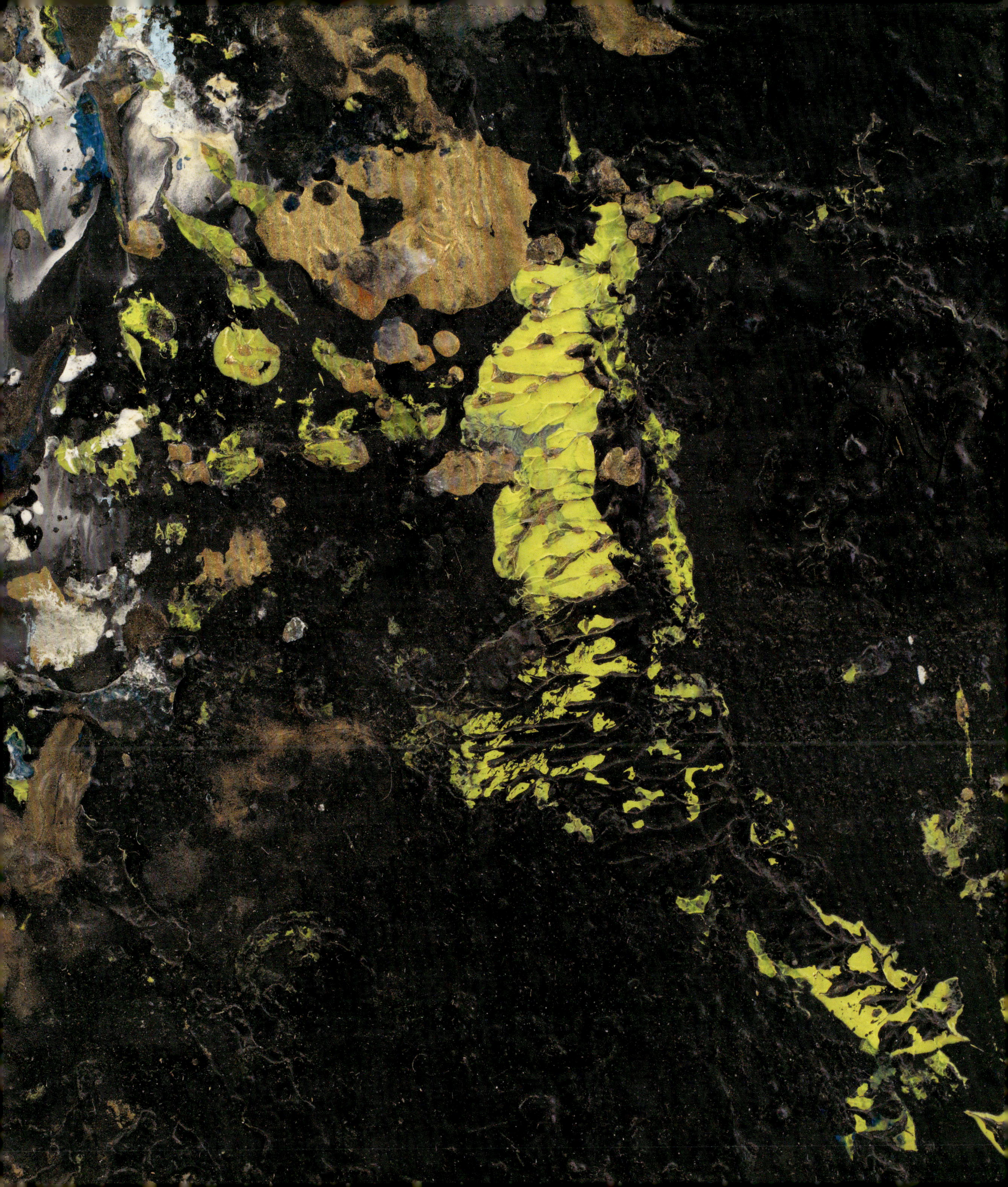

Yellow Amorphous

1950

oil on canvas, 45 $^{1}/_{2}$ x 92"

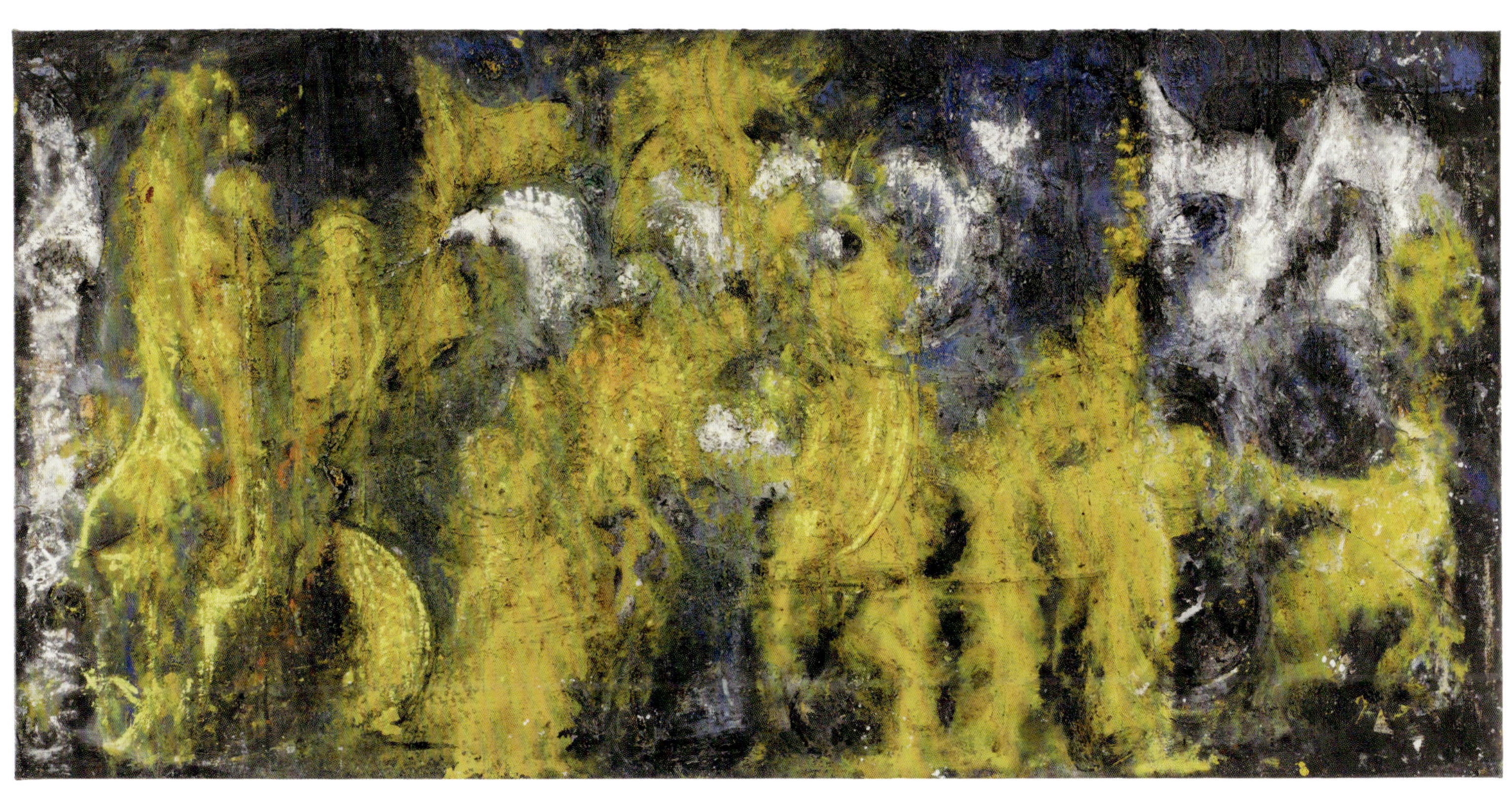

Blue Image

1950

oil on linen, 60 ⁵/₈ x 35 ¹/₄"

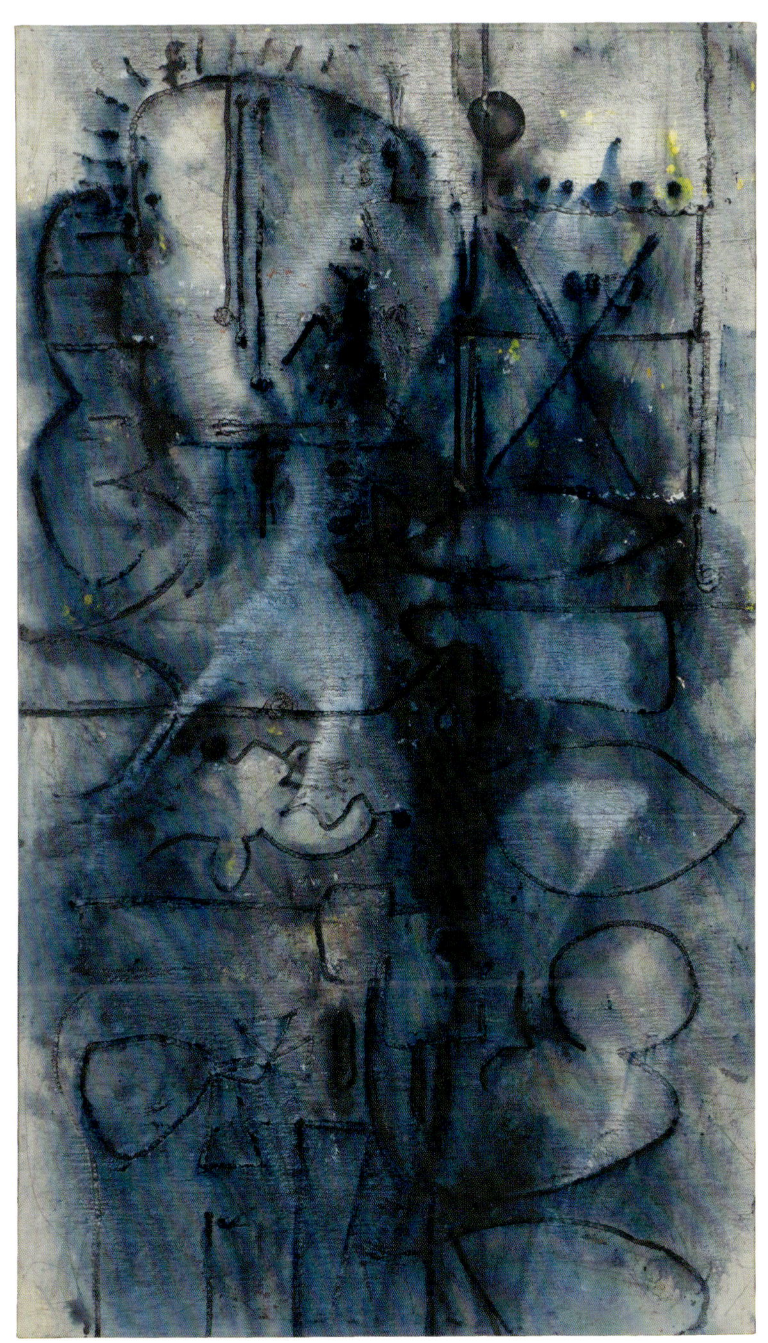

Gothic #2

1951–52

oil on canvas, 60 x 50"

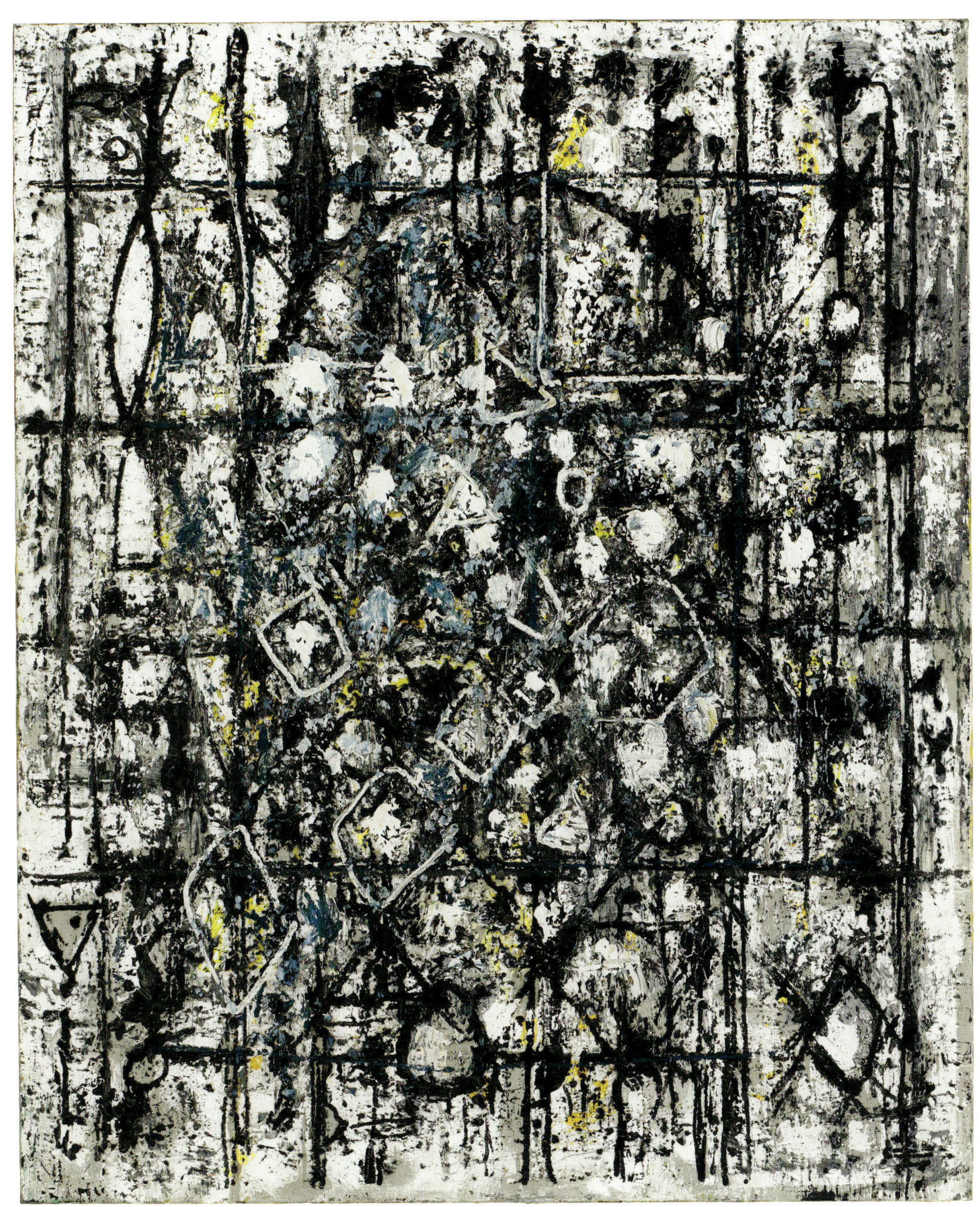

Presence

1956

oil on canvas, 65 ¹/₂ x 44"

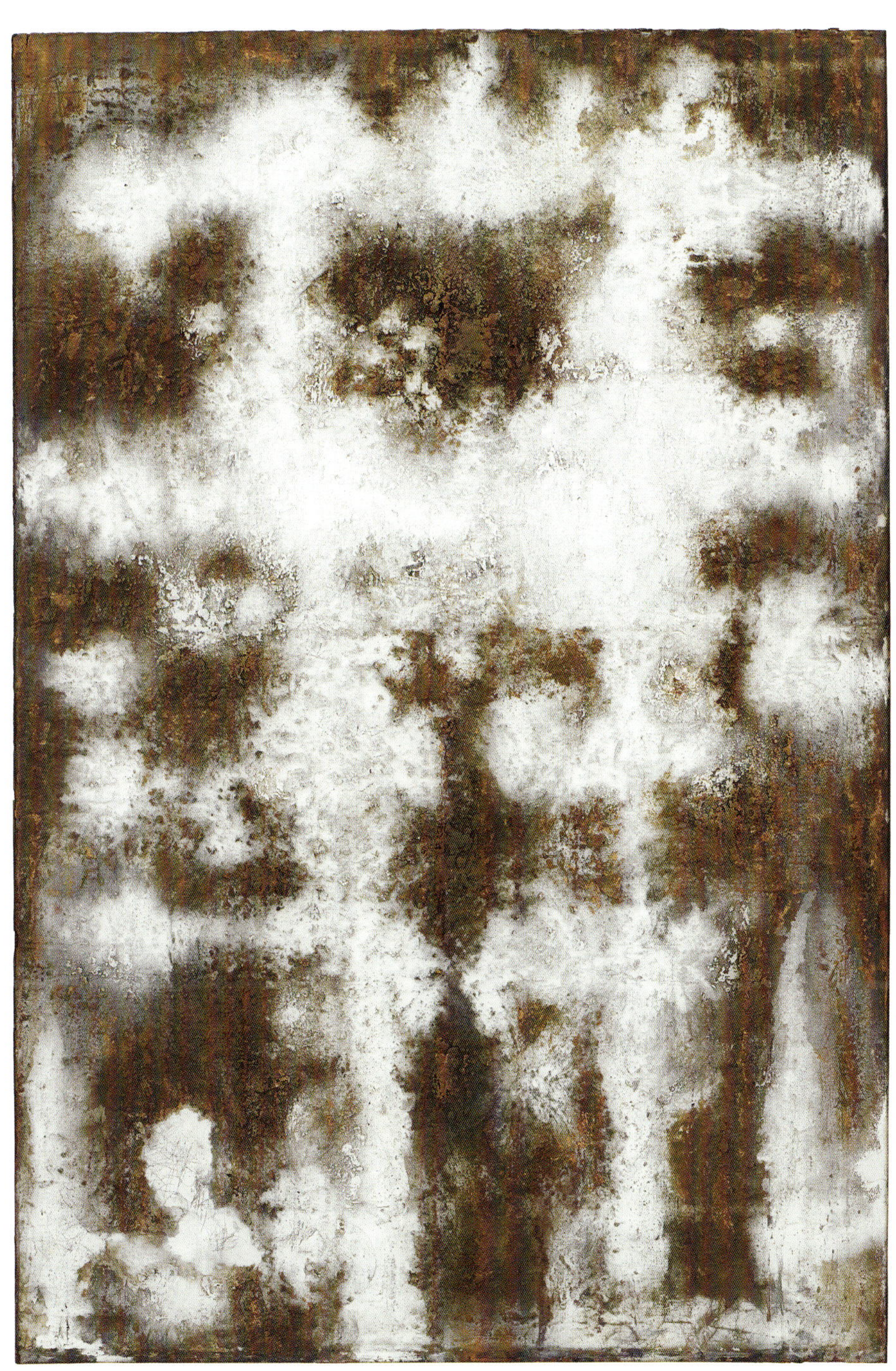

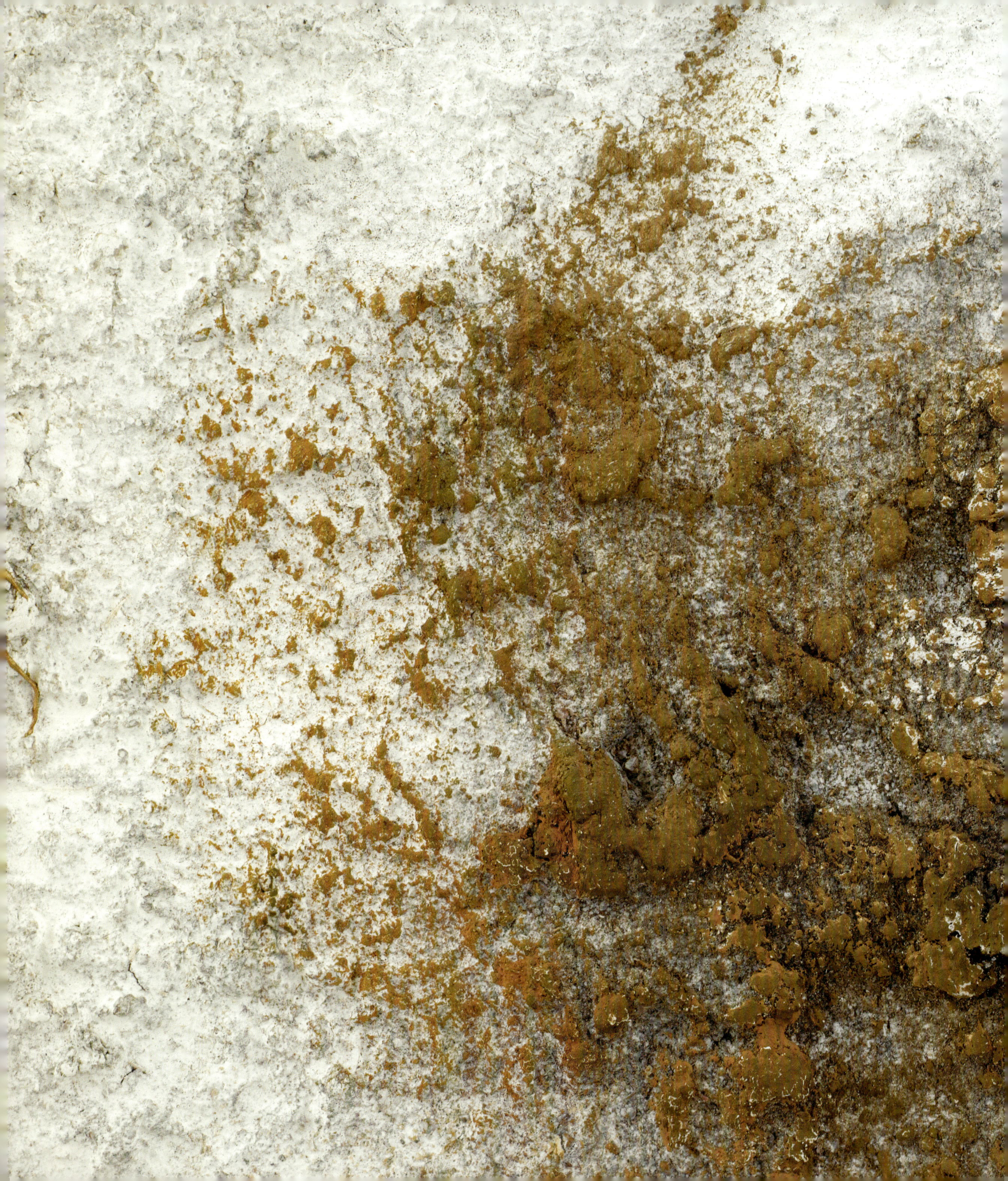

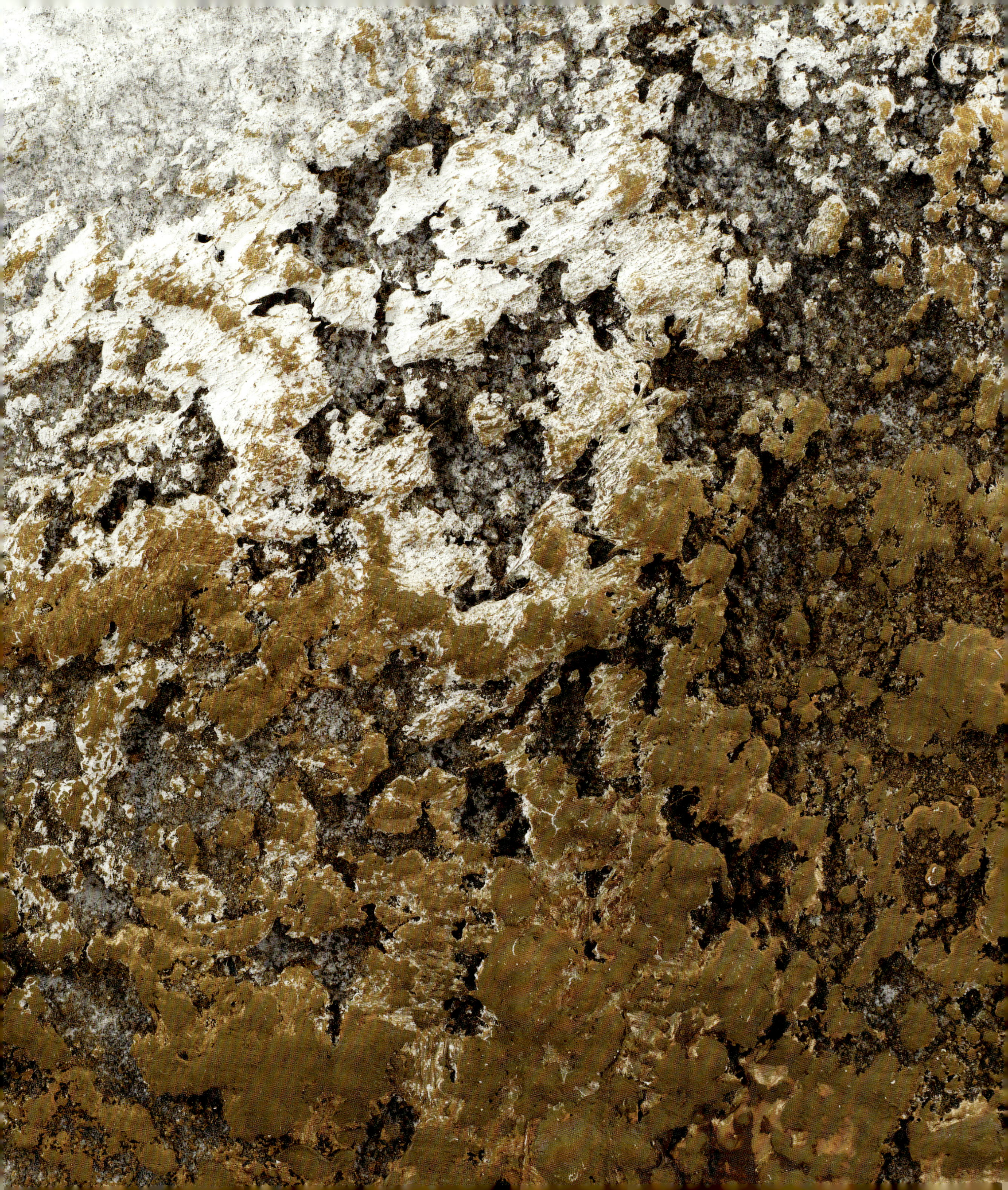

Ossi #2

1958

oil on linen, 57 x 44"

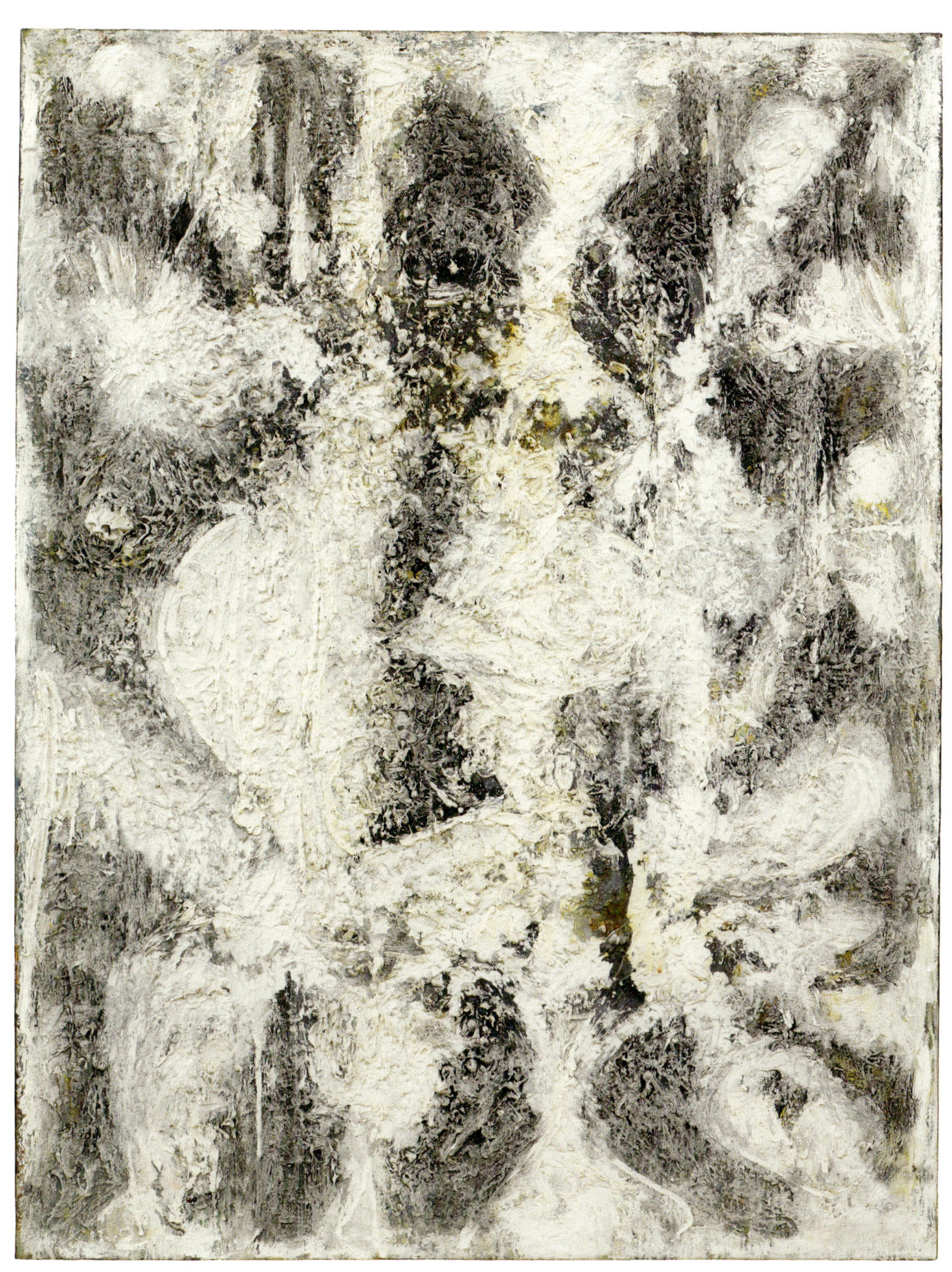

Blue Scroll #2

1958

oil on linen, 56 ½ x 30 ¼"

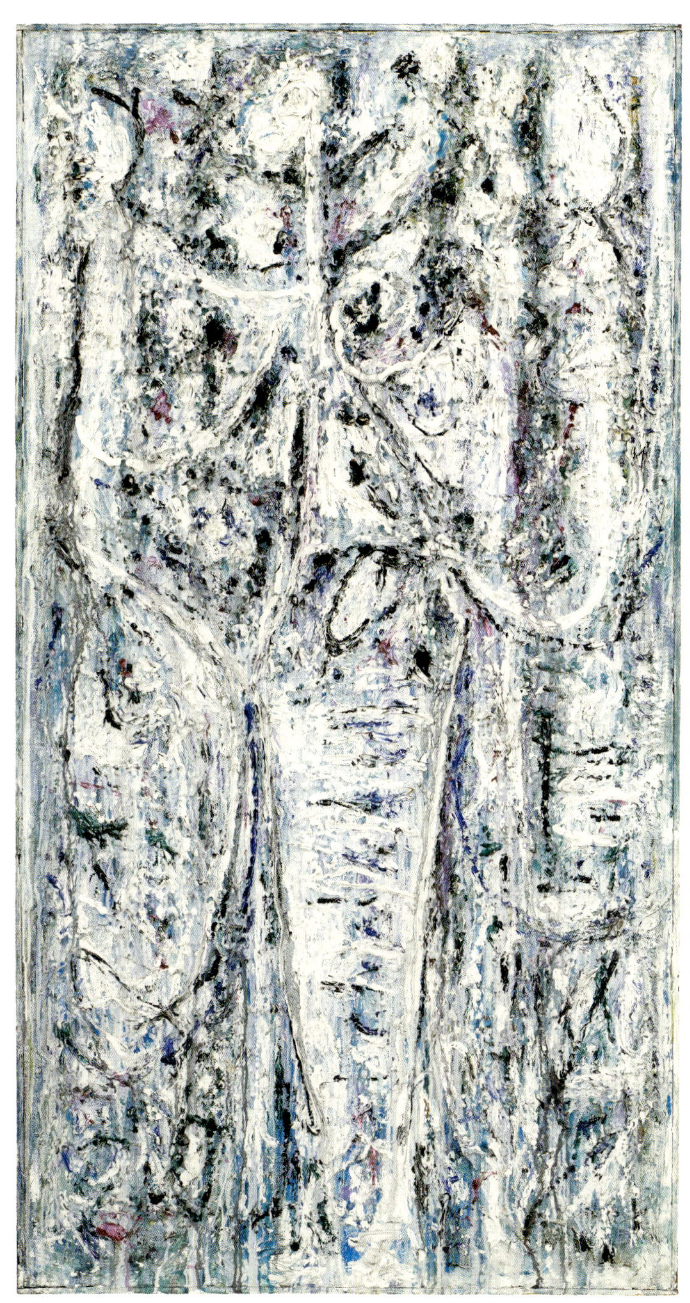

Shadow of the Unknown Bird

1955–58

oil on linen, 95 $\frac{1}{2}$ x 52 $\frac{1}{2}$"

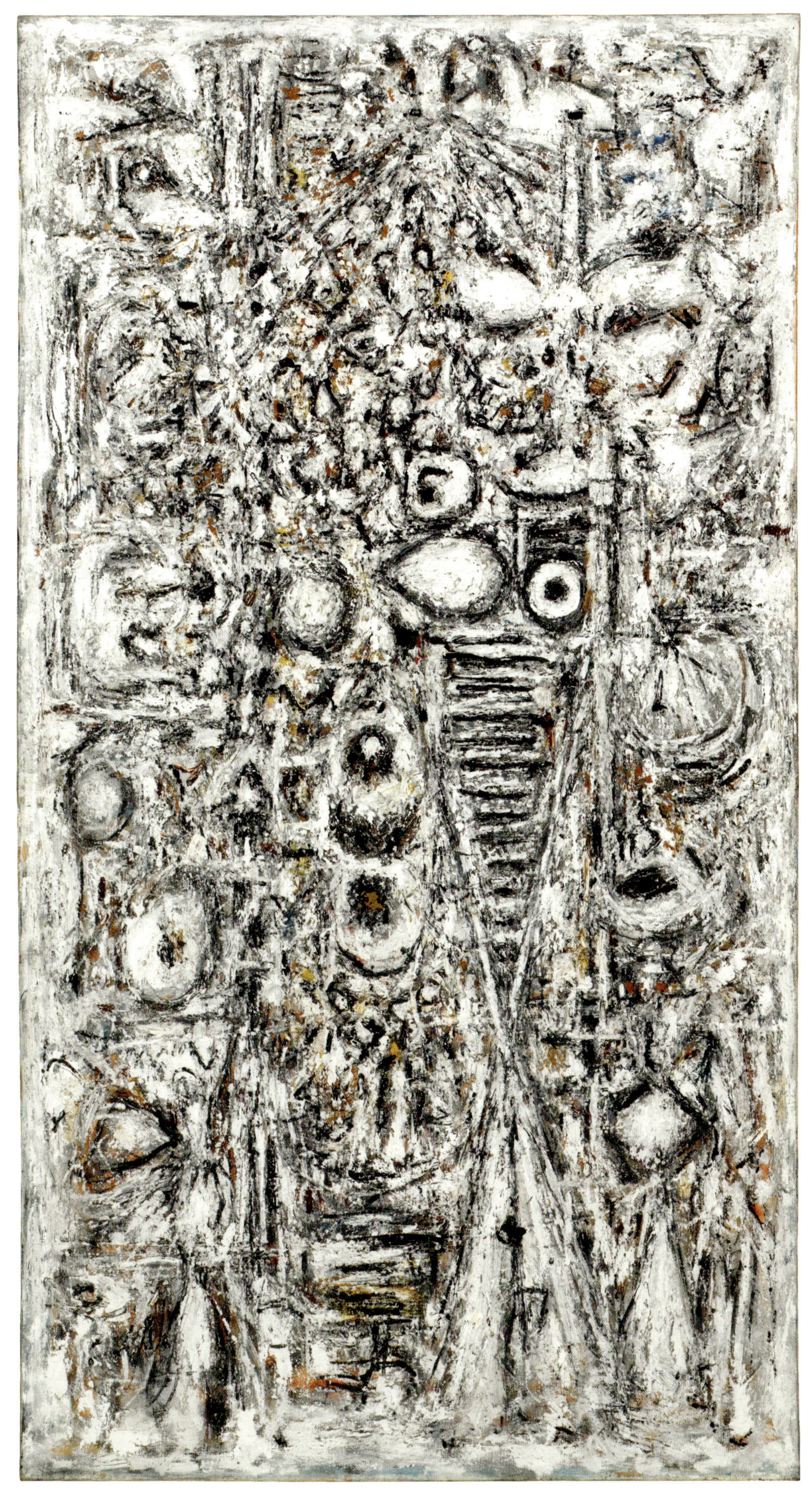

Blue Amorphous #4

1962

oil on canvas, 51 x 75 $\frac{1}{2}$"

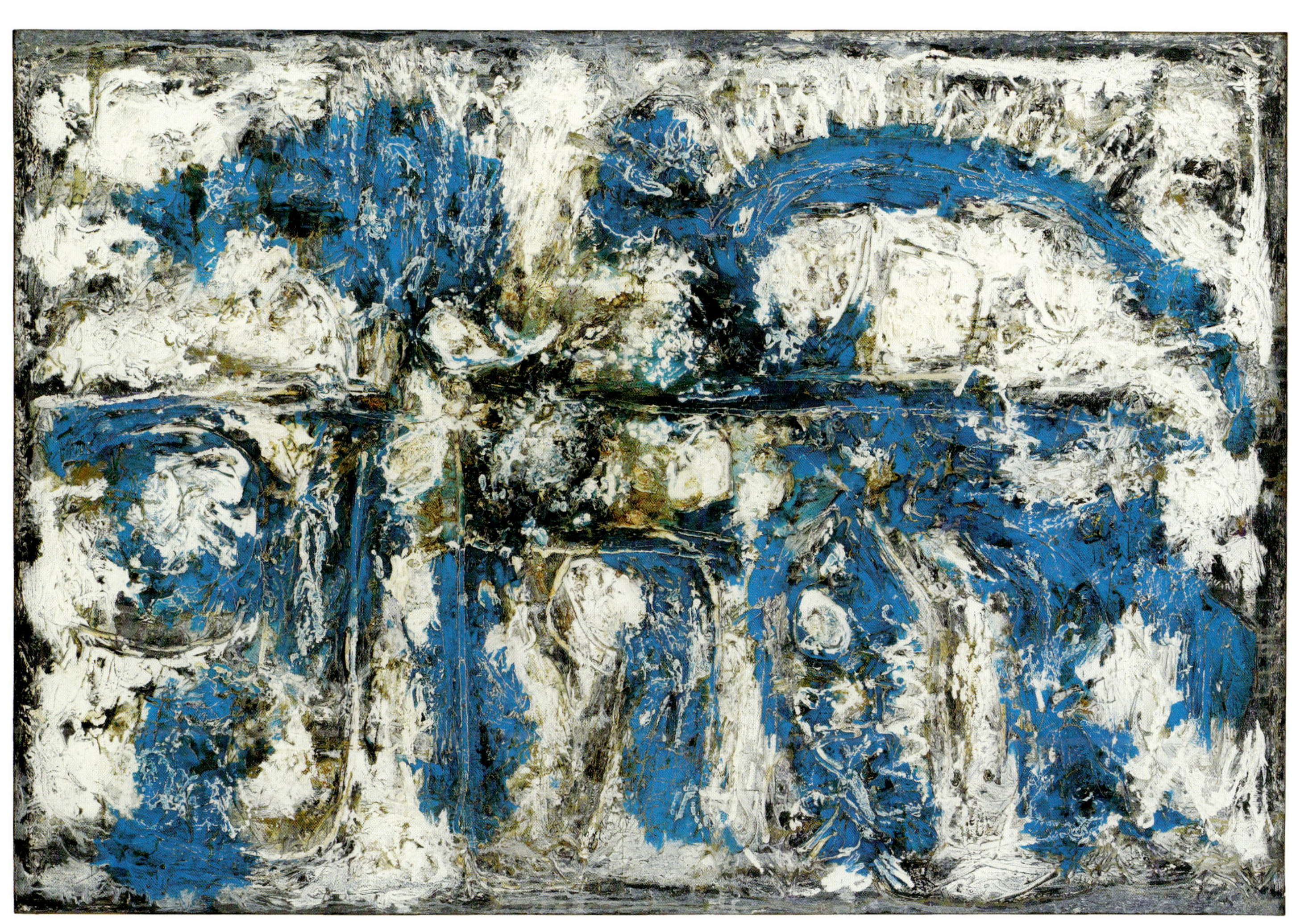

Radiance #1 White

1967

oil on canvas, 80 x 80"

Hieroglyph of Light

1966–67

oil on linen, 43 x 57"

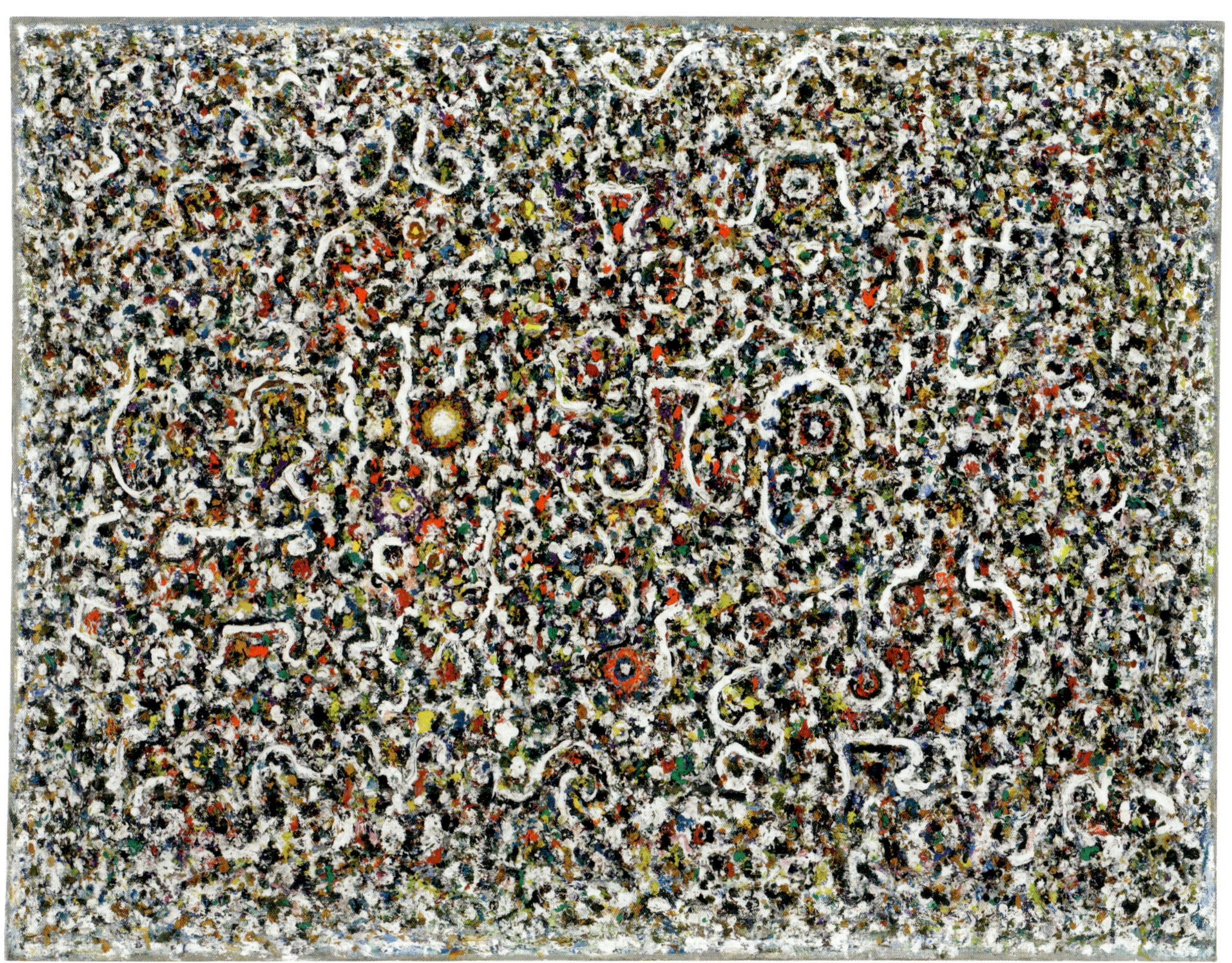

Radiance #3

1968–69

oil on canvas, 72 x 72"

Hieroglyph, Number 2, Black

1974

acrylic on canvas, 90 x 90"

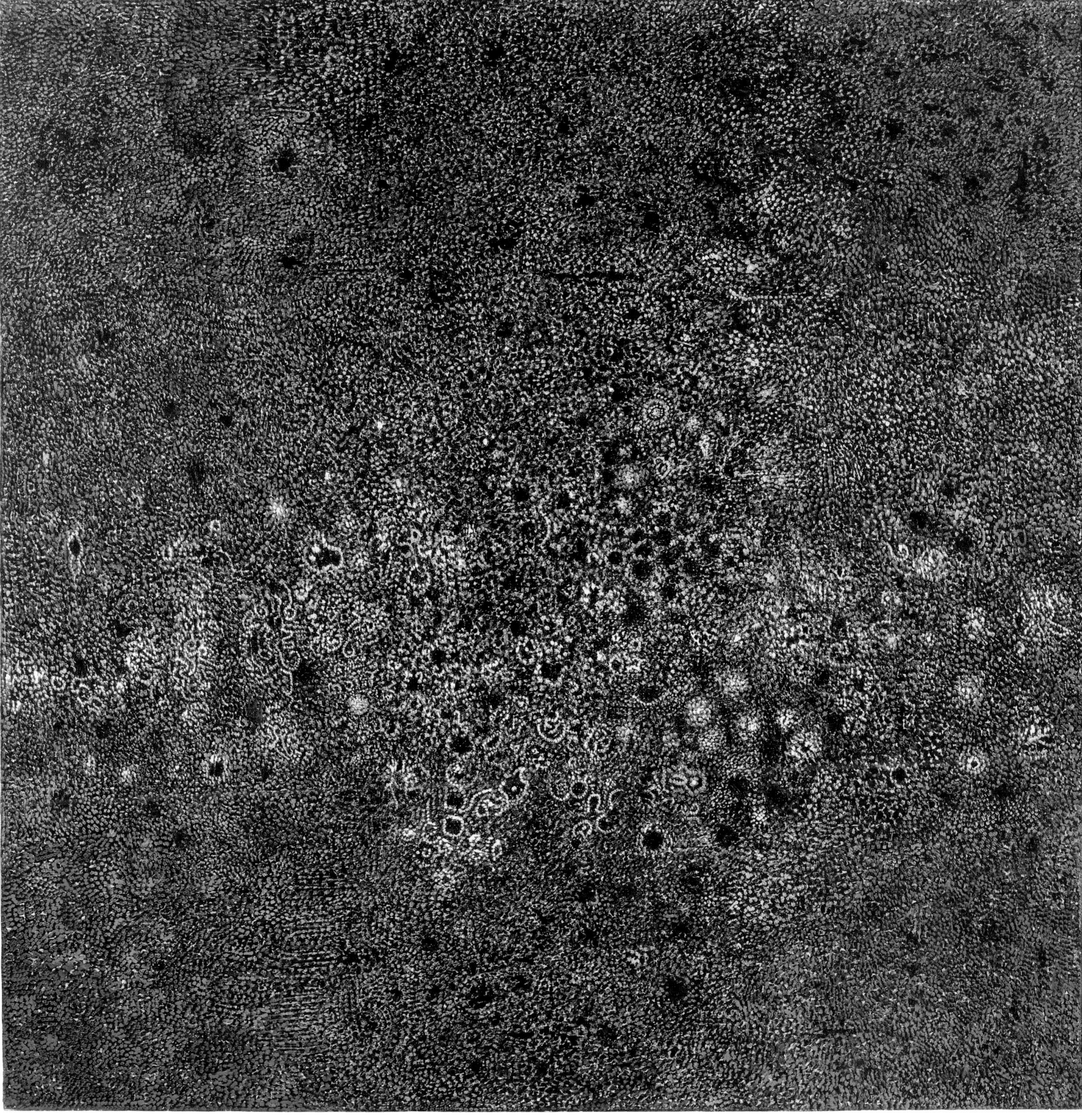

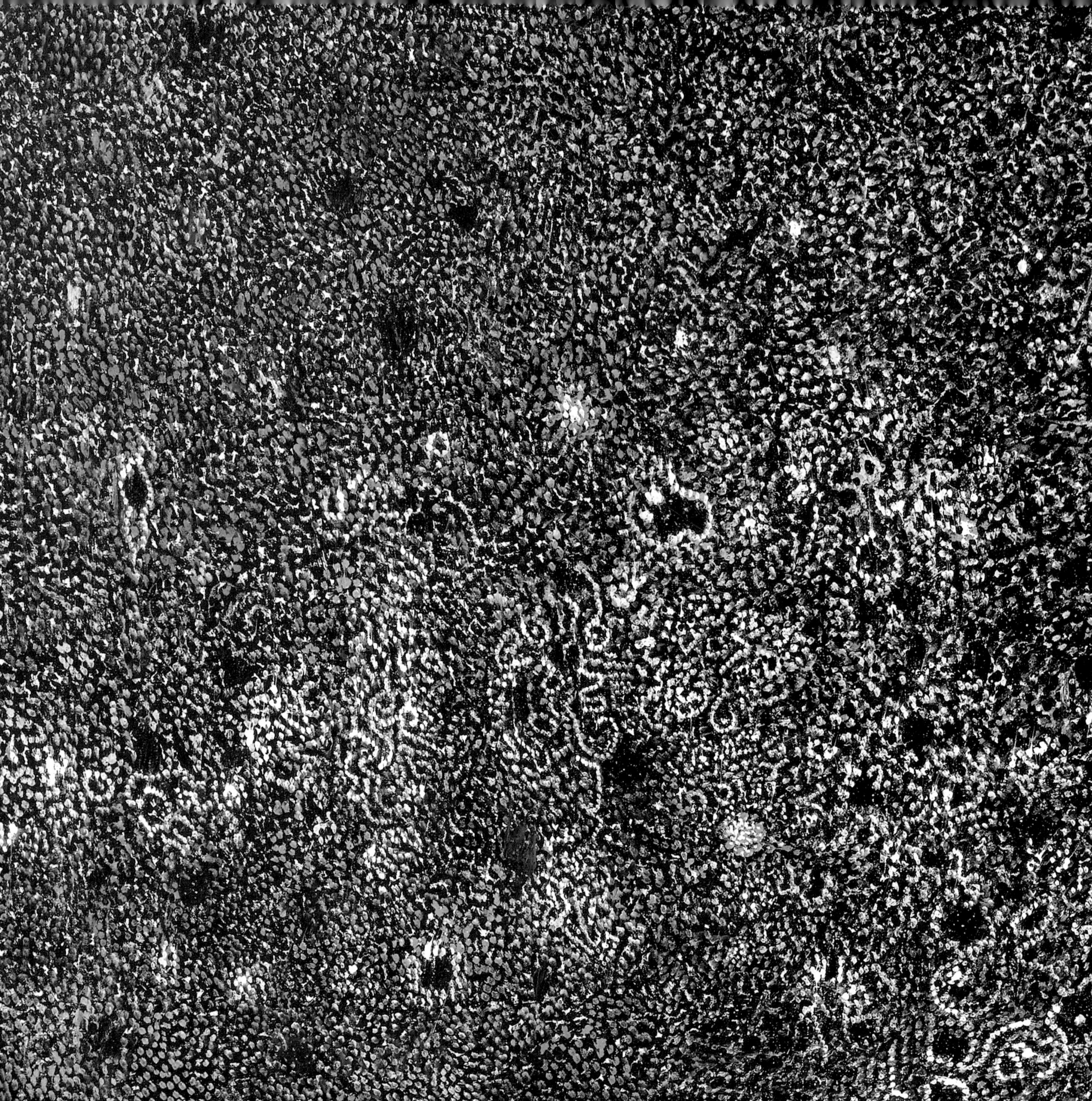

Blue Penetration / Penetration Blue

1975–76

oil on linen, 45 x 58"

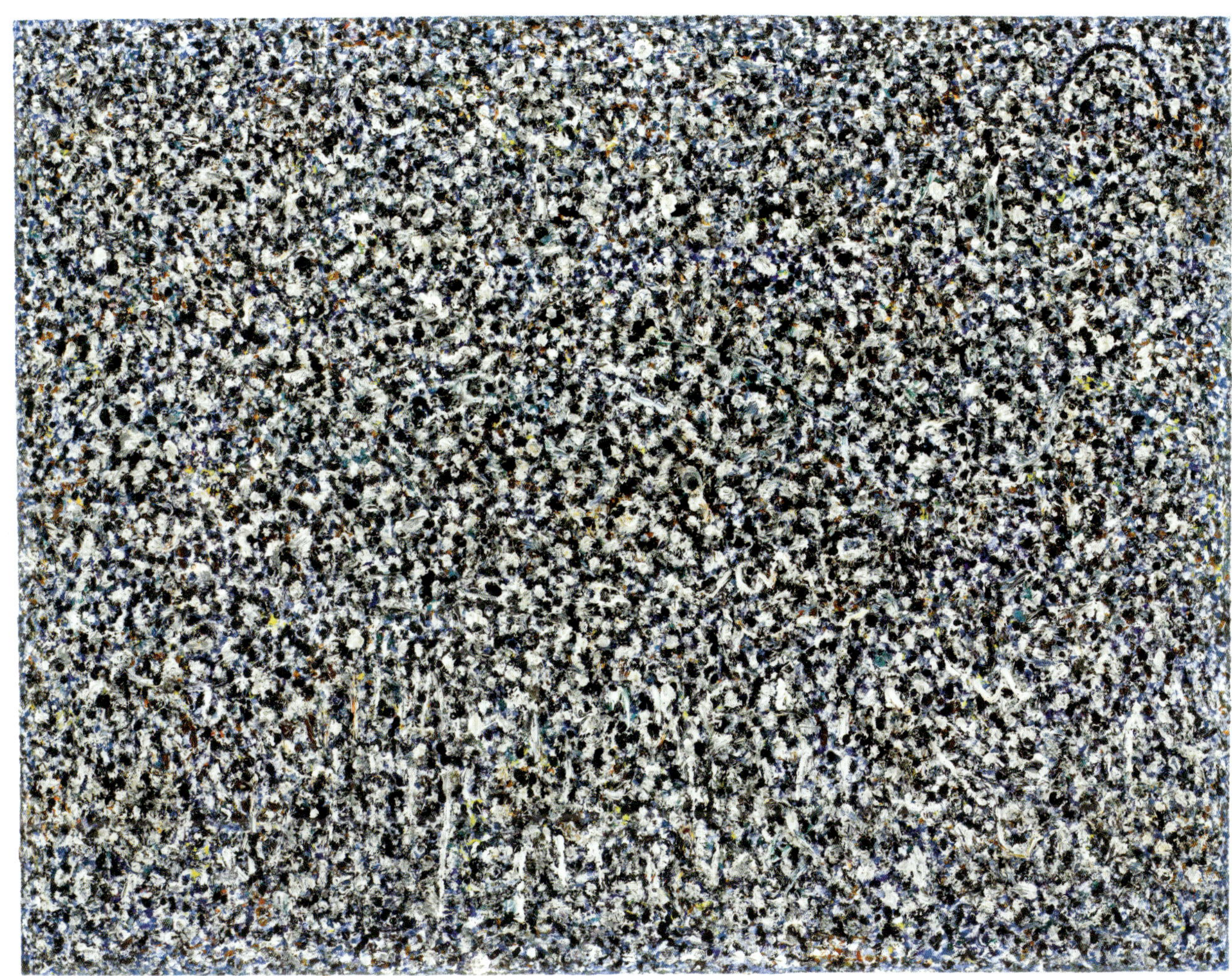

Presence Light

1974–81

oil on linen, 90 x 90"

Soft Edges of Time

1976–82

oil on linen, 54 x 72"

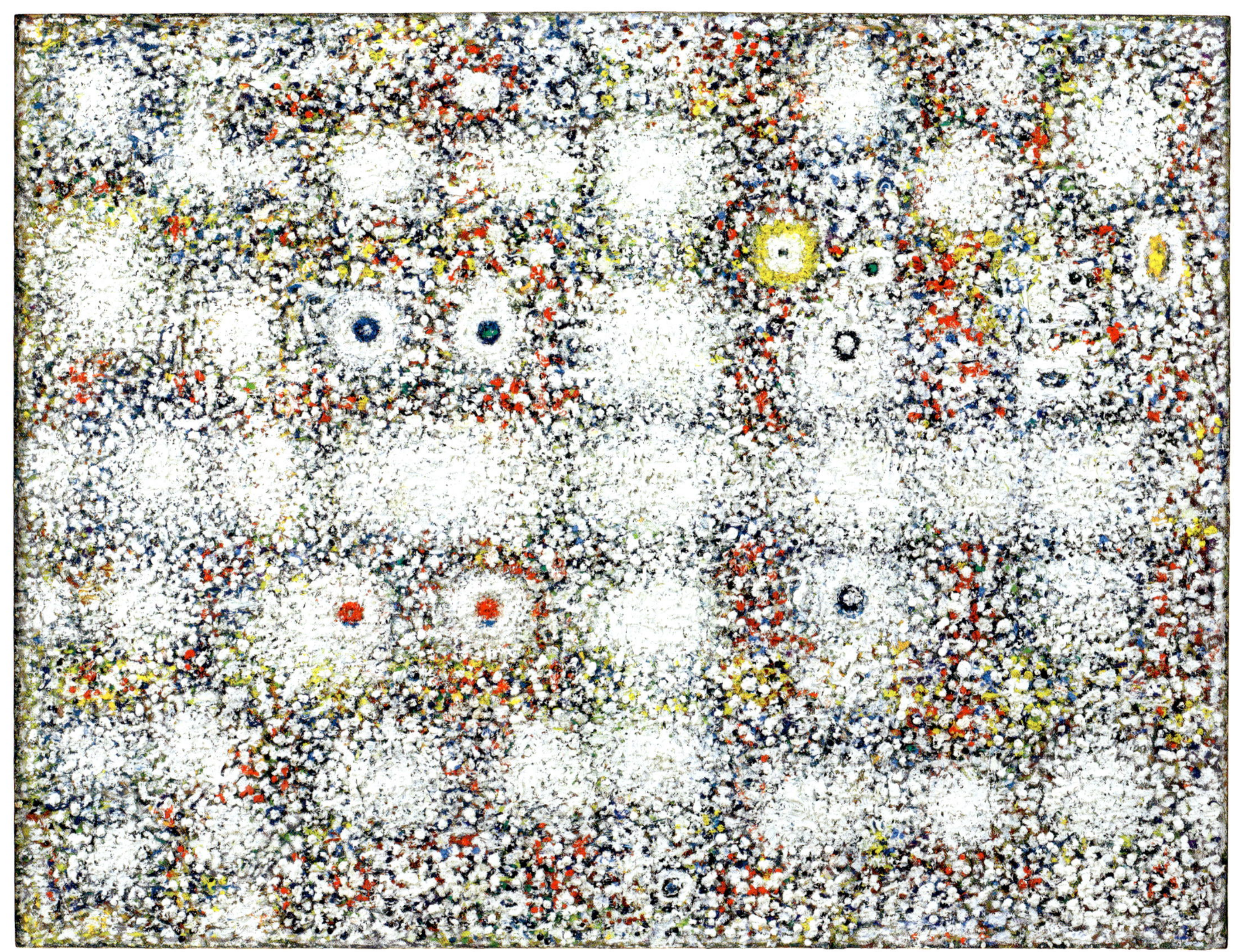

White Silence

1974

acrylic on canvas, 7' 9 ½" x 14' 1 ½"

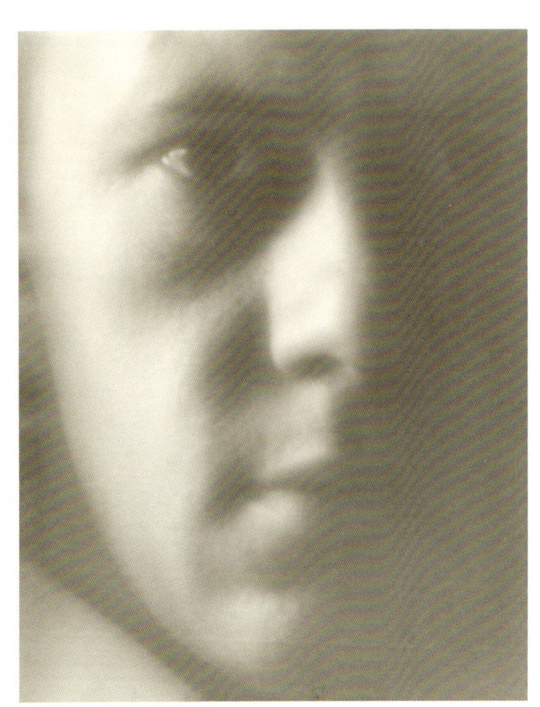

Cover: *White Silence*, 1974 (detail)
Page 14: Richard Pousette-Dart in his studio, Suffern, New York, early 1960s.

Photography:
Tom Barratt; pp. 49–51, 57
Herb Breuer; p. 4
The Estate of Richard Pousette-Dart; pp. 10–11, 62
Fred W. McDarrah / Premium Archive / Getty Images; pp. 14–15
Kerry Ryan McFate; cover and pp. 17, 47, 53–55, 59–60
The Richard Pousette-Dart Foundation; pp. 4, 12–13
The Metropolitan Museum of Art. Image source: Art Resource, NY; pp. 6, 9

Design: Tomo Makiura and Mine Suda

Production: Pace Gallery

Color Correction: Motohiko Tokuta

Printing: Meridian Printing, East Greenwich, Rhode Island

Library of Congress Control Number: 2016949523

ISBN: 978-1-935410-86-7